The Humor Collection

Owain Glyn

The Humor Collection is published under Transcend,
a sectionalized division under Di Angelo Publications
INC.

TRANSCEND

Transcend is an imprint of Di Angelo Publications.
Copyright 2021.
All rights reserved.
Printed in the United States of America.

Di Angelo Publications
4265 San Felipe #1100
Houston, Texas, 77027
www.diangelopublications.com

Library of Congress
The Humor Collection
ISBN: 978-1-955690-17-1

Cover Design:
Internal Layout: Kimberly James
Words by: Owain Glyn

1. Poetry --- Subjects & Themes --- General

United States of America with int. Distribution.

The Humor Collection

Owain Glyn

PART ONE

PART TWO
I'm Not Frightened (Really)

PART ONE

A Homeless Gnome?

I think I may be homeless soon
It seems I'm on my way
I heard that ugly poet git
Discussing it today.
He seems to think I'm useless
A total waste of space
He says these things behind my back
And never to my face.
Well I have got a shock for him,
I see things, and I'm sure,
It wasn't mouth to mouth he gave
That bimbo from next door!!
Then there are the crops he grows,
From really special seed
The law just might be interested
In all this bloody weed!!

A Love Triangle.

I think you know that I love you,
And I thought you loved me too,
But now there's HIM, as well as me,
Instead of two, it seems we're three!
I came to crawl into your bed,
Until I saw his bobbing head,
It hurt so much, I nearly died,
I walked away, and how I cried!
I think you know that it's not fair,
You know that I don't want to share,
Decisions now, need to be made,
Even though I am afraid.
It's up to you, you have to choose,
Even if I have to lose,
It's time for you to clear this fog,
It's either me, or it's that DOG!!

Aunt Aggies' Visit
(The Family Ghost)

Aunt Aggie called the other night,
She asked me where you were,
I told her you had flown the nest,
But you were fine for sure.
She said she might just call on you,
And tell a Christmas tale,
Of times gone past and times to come,
When goodness shall prevail.
So when you blow your candles out,
And rest your weary head,
Remember dear old Aggie,
For she might be by your bed.
Then when you've heard the tale she tells,
Your nightcap you may doff,
But if you didn't like it,
Just tell her to Clear Off!!!

Brain and Cake

I'm quite concerned about my weight
It's been growing fast of late.
I'm having trouble with my clothes
It's my own fault, I must suppose.
I used to think I was quite fit
But now I've got these flabby bits.
If I care to look around
My arse is dragging on the ground.
I think that it must be my age
My tiny brain will not engage.
My fingers tremble over keys
Accompanied, by knocking knees.
I do not want to frighten you
Just because I'm feeling blue
It's just I've had these thoughts before
And, bugger me, I'm twenty four!

ETHELRED

Ethelred had toasted bread
       Each night before he went to bed.
And every day when he got up
       He drank hot chocolate from a cup.

Then before he went to School
       A Bacon Sandwich was the rule.
His Mother made his lunch each day,
       Which took about an hour I'd say.
Two Sausage Rolls and three Pork Pies,
       Four bags of Crisps, as a surprise.
Two Sandwiches of Roasted Lamb,
    A fresh baked Quiche with cheese and ham.
Then for dessert, a chocolate cake,
       With clotted cream she'd always make.

His School was forty yards away,
       A healthy walk, you might just say.
But Ethelred would always stop,
       At McIntyre's, his favourite shop.
Some Sherbet Lemons, or a Dip,
       Into his School Bag he would slip.
Then he would saunter on his way,
       Prepared to face another day.

At School he'd join his Classroom line,
       In readiness to start at nine.
His Mum had written him a note,
       And placed it in his Overcoat.

It asked his Teacher to refrain,
From making him do 'games' again.
"Ethelred's not well" it said,
"Could he do Cookery instead?"

His Teacher thought that it was wise,
In view of his enormous size,
That Ethelred should still take part,
In exercise, to help his heart.
They set off for the Football field,
Where very soon it was revealed,
That Ethelred would still not play,
He'd left his kit at home today.

His Teacher would not be gainsaid,
Nor change the plans that he had made.
Ethelred was much too fat,
And needed help to alter that.
So, off he hauled him to the Gym,
With clear intent, to make him slim.
He'd start him on the Vaulting Horse,
Which he would reinforce, of course.

Then, if Ethelred could cope,
Some time upon the climbing rope.
Young Ethelred looked on, bemused,
His Mother wouldn't be amused,
At Teacher's plans to get him fit,
In fact, she wouldn't hear of it.
He needed building up, she thought,
Not turn into the skinny sort,
Who suffered from perennial ills,

And spent their lives digesting pills.

But Ethelred felt that he should,
        Obey the Teacher, if he could.
So, even though he had no kit,
        Prepared himself to go for it.
He removed his shoes and socks,
        And headed for the vaulting box.

Determinedly, he built up speed,
        Forgetting all about the need,
To leave the ground and make a vault,
        A pretty catastrophic fault!
He hit the box with dreadful force,
        Destroying it, at once, of course.
But even then, he could not stop,
        He hit the wall.......And then went POP!!

And so, a word now, to the wise,
DO NOT MIX FOOD AND EXERCISE!!!

Homes for Gnomes

Would you give a Gnome a home?
Sit him down on sculpted foam?
Find a pleasant shaded spot,
Not too cold, and not too hot?
Somewhere by your goldfish pool,
They do like water, as a rule.
You'll need to keep your pet dog, clear,
Don't want him pissing in his ear.
And if you've got a crazy cat,
You'll need to just get rid of that.
As for the kids, don't be a fool,
Just send them off to private school.
The pleasure you will get is real,
Such happiness, you can't conceal.
A new dimension to your life,
And he won't nag, not like the wife!!
Homes for Gnomes
We bought one, the other day,
To be quite fair, it's in the way.
The bedroom really ain't the place,
To see its grinning, evil face.
Every time that I undress,
I feel it staring, I confess.
It seems to laugh, in measured glee,
Then, it's fishing rod, I see.
So, please, just give this Gnome a home,
I'm sitting here, right by the phone........

In My Mind's Eye

In my mind's eye
I see us walking barefoot
On a soft carpet
Of blue and gold
Through a forest
Of untold beauty.
A unicorn drinks
From a crystal stream,
While happy rabbits
Play with siblings.
Bluebirds chirp
And multi-hued butterflies
Dance on a summer breeze,
Delicate fairies
Play sweet songs
On golden harps.
Suddenly;
A strident voice
Shatters the calm:
"Will you stop that bloody daydreaming,
And go put the trash out!!!!!"
Ah well, they do say marriage is an institution,
I may need an escape plan!

Malady

I saw my quack the other day
And steeled myself for what he'd say
He's quite light-hearted, in his way
But he seemed serious that day.
Let's discuss your malady
I said okay Doc, please feel free
My malady! Of course, of course!
I've sold that car, and bought a Porsche.
The problem is, that with my gout,
I struggle, getting in and out.
So what I do is stand by it,
And look important for a bit!
Listen, Owain, I know best,
And what you need is total rest.
Take this sack of medication,
Even take a long vacation.
Malady
I've organized a nuclear scan
This will help us start to plan.
And if it turns you emerald green
It'll match that hat, which we've all seen.

My Every Need

I see the love shine in your eyes,
It's only then, I realise,
You make the rain clouds all recede,
You fill my each and every need.
Everything I am is you,
I hope you know I love you too.
My life is yours, I have no choice,
But to respond, to your sweet voice.
You guide me to my soft warm bed,
Lay me down, and stroke my head.
So I may dream the sweetest things,
Like squeaky toys, and rubber rings.
And when we go off to the park,
For me to run and have a lark.
I know your love is strong indeed,
When you can trust me, off the lead!!
Woof Woof!

My Hairdresser

I have this guy who cuts my hair
What's left of it, to be quite fair
He always does his very best
He trims the tufts, and shines the rest.
And as he trims, he chats to me
He knows what's going on, you see,
There's nothing he won't know about
He's full of knowledge, without doubt.
Who's screwing whom, and where, and
when
Who's been arrested, once again
Who's got cash, and who has not
On politics, he's plain red hot.
He outdoes the printed news
I'm captivated by his views
My private life, I never leak
Or I'll be in the 'news' next week!!

Ode to a Shopaholic

Oh! Look at those beautiful, beautiful shoes!
I could afford one, but they do come in twos
It would take me a month, if I saved really hard,
I think I might try out my new credit card!

I've tried them both on, and they really look sweet,
But I'll need a new bag, just to make it complete.
That blue one, in leather, has just caught my eye,
They only have one, I will just have to buy!

It's not my fault now, that I need a new dress,
Or the shoes, and the bag, will just look a right mess.
Oh, the dress is just perfect; I'll have to have that,
And you might as well throw in, that gorgeous
red hat.

I'd better stop now, that's enough for today,
I know what my miserable husband will say.
But I know, in my heart, that I'm worth every cent,
And that card's bloody useless, it's now overspent!!

OUR SOVEREIGN

Sixty years upon the Throne
Sword in hand to raise a Knight
Never needed payday loan
Or understood a pauper's plight.

Privileged from birth to Grave
Without a care to cloud the sky
The masses crave a Monarch's wave
With eager voice they all will cry;

"God save the Queen, God save the King
"God save the Prince of Wales"
We don't mind if they're Germans
Even Greeks, if all else fails!

We don't want bloody Paddys
Or the Taffies or the Scots
History has warned us
They're a load of drunken Sots!

Forget about the Africans
Their skin's a funny colour
And Muslims wouldn't work at all
We'd end up with a Mullah!

No, real Monarchs must be white
With blood that's truly blue
I've checked mine and it's all Red
I expect that yours is too.

We were born as subjects
To bend low and know our place
We should be bloody grateful
Just to gaze upon that face.

That they should spend our hard earned cash
Is but their Royal right
Lackeys wake them up each day
And tuck them in at night.

They need their Gold-Lined Palaces
Their Castles give them joy
They can hide their indiscretions
And keep out the Hoi Polloi.

But of course they bring in Tourists
With their Dollars and their Yen
Who never catch a glimpse of them
So back they come again.

We love our Royal family
They make us feel secure
We don't mind if they cost us
Fifty million every year!

So sixty years of service
Is a feat to celebrate
We'll get an extra day off work
It's what makes Britain Great!!!!

SUNDAY SCHOOL

Sit still, I need to wash your face, you can't go out like this,

What would the neighbors think?

That I would let you go to Chapel to gaze on the countenance of our Saviour

With a dirty face?

Sit still, I need to wash your ears, you can't go out like this,

What would the Mrs. Pugh think?

That I would let you go to Chapel to hear the word of our Saviour

With dirty ears?

Sit still, I need to wash your hands, you can't go out like this,

What would Mrs. Evans think?

That I would let you go to Chapel to touch the words of our Saviour

With dirty hands?

Sit still, I need to wash your knees, you can't go out like this,

What would Mrs. Thomas think?

That I would let you go to Chapel to kneel to the Glory of our Saviour

With dirty knees?

Oh, sod, I've run out of soap, why don't you stay at home,

And play instead of pray?

Resident Evil

As I approach the dark, almost threatening,
house

I feel the prescience of impending doom.

While I walk the silent pathway,

I notice that the previously lush lawn,

Is black.

Roses wilt on their vines,

Hydrangeas sadly droop.

As I enter the dank hallway,

The marrow in my bones chills.

Blood, almost black with age,

Drips down the walls.

The silence is deafening.

With intense trepidation

I open a creaking door.

My wife sits, stiff backed,

Almost frozen in time.

Through a thin smile

She says,

"My Mother's come to stay

"For a few days

Isn't that nice??"

Tamara

A snow white pillow, filled with down
For you to rest your head
And you may lay your silken form
Upon this tousled bed.
As I lay silent, next to you
And gaze into your eyes
I can see a love that's true
And then I realize.
That I am blessed, your curves to stroke
To feel your warm sweet breath
To know, how you, my love awoke
To stay with me till death
And as we lie, in ecstasy
A voice comes from above.......
"Have you got that bloody Dog on the bed again?"
"I've told you, it's not hygienic!!"

Walkies!

THE CAT

I saw that Cat the other day,

Where he was going who could say?

He strode along his head held high, his tail;
erect, to brush the sky.

He looked at me with pure disdain,

As if to say "Not you again!"

His promenading, full of grace, would
indicate he owns the place.

What does he really think he's at?

Can he not see he's just a Cat?

And be satisfied with that?

Oh no, this feline bon-viveur,

Of royal bloodline he is sure,

How can he be the stuff of Kings, while
eating Rats and Things with wings?

His gait screams immortality,

Nine lives he has, supposedly,

But that old tale is just a myth, not
something that I'm bothered with.

His haughty ways do not fool me,

I see through him with clarity,

He's just another quadruped, with dreams
of glory in his head.

He pads along with studied poise,

His ears pricked for any noise,

Which might just help him demonstrate,

those hunting skills he thinks innate.

He's self deluded,

Self possessed,

But all the same, a Cat, at best.

He turned the corner of my street,

The tour of his domain complete,

Adventures over for a while, he headed for his domicile.

I sauntered home with confidence,

To find him perched upon my fence,

I picked him up and tickled him, he purred at me and we went in.

THE HANGOVER

When I got up this morning
It was almost yesterday
Though it could have been tomorrow
I just really couldn't say.

My head was facing back to front
My nose seemed upside down
My eyebrows stuck together
In an imbecilic frown.

My legs had all the feeling
You'd expect from frozen peas
Which was further complicated
By the loss of both my knees.

And when I tried to focus
On a point in time and space
My eyes just fled their sockets
At a most alarming pace.

Now what had caused this crisis
Which had left me all but dead
Screwing up my faculties
And messing up my head?

Fourteen pints of Real Ale
Could well provide a clue
Especially when they're followed
By some Double Whiskeys too.

I don't suppose the Curry
Will have helped an awful lot
I can't remember what it was
But it was Bloody Hot!

I closed my eyes against the light
To block out all the pain
And prayed for equilibrium
So I could try again.

I felt quite dehydrated
So I crawled off to the sink
To fill myself with H2o,
Simplicity, you'd think.

But my attempts to hold the glass
Were clearly bound to fail
My body shook from head to foot
Way off the Richter scale.

Just then a can of Speckled Hen
Came slowly into view
Hairs and Dogs sprang to my mind
And it was liquid too!

I drank it down in just one go
It seemed to hit the spot
The shakes were now subsiding
It was helping quite a lot.

My eyes began to focus
And my head began to clear

I thanked the Gods for hairy dogs
Normality was near.

I quickly took a shower
Then I scraped my prickly face
I shoved a brush inside my mouth
To fumigate the place.

My eyes still looked quite bleary
And my face looked very pale
But I thought I knew the answer
A few pints of Abbot Ale

I'd considered, very briefly
Should I join the Temperance Club?
But since I'm not too social
I'll just stroll down to the Pub!

THE REVOLUTION

"The Peasants are revolting, Sire! They're
not so far away"

"What of the bloody Pheasants, man,
whose Pheasants did you say?"

"I said that it was PEASANTS, Sire, they're
not too far away"

"Well tell them I can't see them now, my
Tailors' on his way"

"I don't think they will listen, Sire, they've
got no food to eat,

"They've got no clothes upon their backs,
or shoes upon their feet."

"You mean to say they're naked, man,
that's very indiscreet,"

"Go and fetch some Quails' eggs and some
Roast Flamingo meat."

"But what about the Peasants, Sire, they're
almost at the gate?"

"Throw them bread and dripping, man, and
say they'll have to wait."

"I don't think that will help, Sire, they're all
fired up with hate,

"They think you're pretty out of touch and
past your sell-by date."

"Then call the Palace Guard out, man, it's
what I pay them for

"Once they've shot a few of them, they won't come back for more."

"The Palace Guard is fleeing, Sire, they're heading for the door,

"They've thrown away their rifles and the uniforms they wore."

"I'll have their heads, I really will, It's Treason, don't you know,

"And after all I've done for them, that they should treat me so."

"If you want my advice, Sire, I think that you should go,

"It could be suicidal, Sire, to hold the Status Quo."

"Alright, then get my jewels, which are underneath my bed,

"Don't put them in the Limousine we'll use the Ford instead.

"Who is that behind you, man, his clothes all stained in red?

"He seems to be quite angry; he's just chopped off my head!"

Will that be all, Sire?

The Temperance Club

A Welshman and two Irishmen
Went into a Pub
Said Patrick to the barman
"Is this the Temperance Club?"

"Of course it's not, you Leprechaun
"What we sell is Beer."
"Okay we might just have one
"Now that we are here."

Well, one turned into many
And they lost all track of time
The Beer was just like nectar
And the pickled eggs, sublime.

They fell to playing Poker
Throwing cash into the pot
The Welshman had a Royal Flush
And so he won the lot.

When it came to closing time
The barman threw them out
The Temperance Club was closed by now
Of that there was no doubt.

Instead they found another club
Where ladies got undressed
Patrick said, "Just look at them!"
The Welshman was impressed.

They handed over money
And found a grubby chair
Bought some very bad champagne
And watched the ladies bare.

But they ran out of money
And the doorman made them leave
Now they had to walk back home
And make their wives believe.

They'd spent the day in abstinence
And truly signed the pledge.
Instead of smelling like a still
And crawling through a hedge.

Things did not go quite as planned
Their wives were not amused
They felt as if they'd been let down
In fact, they felt abused.

Decisions must be taken
Of that there was no doubt
And after much discussion
Their wives just threw them out.

If in your weaker moments
You decide to give up drink
Imagine sleeping in the park
And have another think!!

THOUGHTS

I think I do,
But then I don't,
I think I will,
But then I won't
I think I might,
But then might not,
I feel I should,
But have I got
The time and space,
To be quite sure,
Or should I really,
Take some more?
So, what I'll do,
Is wait a bit,
And take the time,

To think on it!!!

Vegetable Abuse (Celery)

I knew a man who merrily
Took whisky with his celery
He thought it an efficient way
To help toward his five a day.

And, of course, he'd get a drink
A pleasant two-in-one, you'd think
But things did not work well, you see
The celery just made him pee.

Then his nose and ears turned green
Followed quickly by his spleen
These were not the only troubles
His pee came out in small green bubbles.

He asked his Doctor to decide
If this was caused by pesticide
His Doctor very soon agreed
A remedy was clear, indeed.

Keep up the whisky, merrily
But cut down on the celery
The root cause of this foul affliction
Was down to celery addiction!

Please consume celery responsibly.

The Visit

I perambulate
Slowly,
My feet move
Robotically,
With no help from me.
My heart beats
Like a kettle drum
In an empty cavern.
Pushing congealing blood
Through resistant veins.
Sinews, taught,
Like barbed wire
Ripping at muscle,
And flesh alike.
My hands, hanging limp,
One grasps a dark flask
Of dark red viscous
liquid.
Above,
A sullen sky
Threatens.
I approach a dark forbidding door,
Tug on a rope.
Inside bells crash
Through empty halls.
The door creaks open,
There stands
A vision
Of pure malevolence.

I find my voice,
And rasp,

"Hello Mother-in-Law,

"I've brought your Sherry.

Constant Inconstancy

You rise again, so phoenix like, dead
ashes into flames,
But now I have your measure, I won't
play your cruel games.
I sit alone and stare at walls; my mind is
filled with you,
But constancy is not your style, it's
something you eschew.

You don't come home for days on end,
Then turn up like a ghost.
And when you rest upon my chest,
That's when I love you most.

One day you have eyes of fire,
The next you're cold as ice.
If you wish to stay with me,
Then take this sound advice;
If you don't start to behave, I'm going to
nail up that catflap!!!!!!!

The Mirror

We've got this mirror in the hall,
I don't use it much at all,
Maybe once or twice a day,
If I'm passing by that way.

I just check I'm well presented,
That's why mirrors were invented.
It's important to look good,
My mother always said I should.

My hair is soft and brushed in place,
There are no age lines on my face.
My eyes are soft and both in line,
My nose is regal, aquiline.

My body's lithe and really sleek,
I've got the curves that most boys seek.
I know how to swing my hips,
And run my tongue across my lips.

I'm still not perfect, that I know,
And it gets worse each month I grow.
I've got these spots upon my face,
And almost every other place.

They're on my back, and on my face,
And almost every other place.
It fills me full of deep frustration,
Who'd want to be a girl DALMATION???

Please Come Be My Valentine

Will you be my Valentine?
I'm really, really, hot.
I live in a large mansion
And own a super yacht.
I drink champagne for breakfast,
I eat oysters for my tea.
I have a load of servants,
Who do everything for me.
Not everything is perfect
I'm sure that you won't mind,
I've got a very loving heart,
And I'm very kind.
My nose fell off last Wednesday,
It really was a shock.
I found it underneath the bed
And keep it in my sock.
You'll have to speak quite loudly
I only have one ear.
My teeth fell out on Thursday,
I'd better make it clear.
Some other bits are missing,
But we'll not go into that.
My hair fell out on Thursday,
But I've got a wicked hat!
So, come on, take a chance on me,
Regret it you will not.
My temperature is off the scale,
I told you I was hot!!

Be My Valentine

Will you be my Valentine?
On this auspicious day?
I really need a Valentine,
Who does things just my way.
Please come be my Valentine,
I think you're very sweet.
I really want a Valentine
Prepared to wash my feet.
I hope you'll be my Valentine,
Walk doggy in the rain,
I need the kind of Valentine
Who rarely will complain.
I'm hoping for a Valentine
Who'll show she really cares.
I need a helpful Valentine,
Who'll help me up the stairs.
If you are my Valentine,
You'll have a love sublime.
You will not see a lot of me,
I'm sleeping all the time.

PART TWO
I'm Not Frightened (Really)

Marie is searching for love.

Her satnav does not seem to be helping.

Nor do her dysfunctional family.

Add to that her band of lunatic Poets.

And we're in for a wild ride!

Episode One: A Boyfriend's Tale

I'll meet you by your garden gate
I'll come at eight, I won't be late
I will not knock upon your door
Your father answered it before.

He slowly looked me up and down
His face congealed into a frown
" I don't want any, go away
"And don't come back another day!"

"I'm here to see Marie," I said
And proudly lifted up my head
I thought that if I stood my ground
He'd think me brave and come around.

Instead he said, "What's on your head?
"Is it alive, or is it dead?"
"No, that's my hair, sir," I replied
He laughed so much he almost cried.

I'd spent a mint on styling gel
And put some highlights in, as well
For him to castigate my hair
Was very rude, and most unfair.

Then he started on my clothes
"Where the hell did you buy those?"
I would have said " A high street shop"
But he was laughing fit to pop.

I couldn't see things getting better
Standing there, just getting wetter
Did I not say that it was raining?
Honestly, I'm not complaining.

I turned and left, respectfully
I heard him laugh, hysterically
So, I'll meet you by your gate
I'll come at eight, I won't be late.

Episode Two: A Father's Tale

"Marie, my princess, can we speak?
 "About your latest little geek?"
You know I want the best for you,
A handsome Prince, who's strong and true.

When I opened up the door
I was shocked by what I saw
His hair was bleached, and strangely spiked
I saw nothing that I liked.

His dress was weird, and quite unkempt
My first impression was contempt
And when he said he'd called for you
My self control, well it just blew.

I might have laughed, okay, I did
The thought of you, and this weird kid
I only want the best for you
You're still quite young, at forty two.

Episode Three: A Mother's Tale

Marie, it's no good you telling me
Your problems with your Dad, you see
It's not as if he's truly bad
It's just that he is barking mad.

You only have yourself to blame
You never learn, it's such a shame
Remember Rob, or was it Bob?
You know the one without a job?

Your father tried hard not to fail
Till he found out he'd been in jail
Then there was that midget chap
Who got your Dad in such a flap.

He couldn't look him in the eye
He had to kneel to even try
You really do not help yourself
By moaning you are on the shelf.

Find a boy who's kind and smart
Who dresses well, and doesn't fart
Who'll love you, dear, and treat you well
Who won't use drugs, and doesn't smell.

Now, if you want some free advice
Before you bring them home, think twice
Why not meet them at a dance?
At least you'd start with half a chance!

Episode Four: A Brother's Tale

Our Marie, she drives me mad
She's always rowing with my Dad
And then she's crying on the phone
I'm living in a hostile zone.

She brought home some guy named Lloyd
Now there was one that you'd avoid
His voice was real high pitched and loud
His dandruff hung there like a cloud.

He dressed a lot like Liberace
Claimed he'd bought it from Versace
He might have got away with that
If he had not been quite so fat.

His flesh poked out of several holes
His stomach settled down in rolls
But, I think, what finished it
Were his attempts to try and sit.

He breathed in, deeply, shook his hair
Then bent his frame to meet the chair
What happened next? I think you'll guess
Suffice to say, the chair's a mess.

That's the problem with Marie
She doesn't think sufficiently
One day, maybe, she will see
There's a cost to love, it isn't free.

My Dad thinks she's predatory
And she should be more like me
Who's soft, and kind, in every way
I haven't told him that I'm Gay!! (Yet)

Episode Five: A Sister's Tale

I've got a sister called Marie
She has to share a room with me
She's not what you'd call clean and neat
Then there's this problem with her feet.

I open windows, spray the place
And wear a medic's mask, in case
The Doctor's right it could just spread
I've had to fumigate her bed.

She also borrows all my clothes
I shouldn't mind though, I suppose
Daddy says not to be mean
But I'm size eight, and she's sixteen!!!

He says that if she meets a man
She might leave home, and then I can
Have my room back all to myself
And she can climb down off the shelf.
I think he might be dreaming!!!

Episode Six: An Auntie's Tale

I have this niece, she's called Marie
She wants to come and stay with me
She tells me things are really bad
She cannot get on with her Dad.

But I've a problem, with a lodger
Real nice guy, his name is Roger
Says he wants to rearrange
His gender even though it's strange.

He likes to wear my underwear
Which I don't mind, I do not care
I love him coz he's really cute
Forget the clothes, there's no dispute.

So, if I really have to choose
He will win and she will lose!!

Episode Seven: Marie Fights Back

I guess that you've all heard of me
I'm that girl, you know, Marie
That Poet's filled you full of rhymes
All about my life and times.

He's sold you rhymes about my brother
Then my Auntie, and my Mother
Made my Father look quite mad
Making out my love life's bad.

Well, I have joined a dating site
Who've guaranteed me Mr. Right
So in a week, or maybe two
I'll show this Poet who is who.

He really needs to get a life
I wonder if he's got a wife??
I think that deep down, secretly
He's probably in love with me! (We'll see)

Episode Eight: Marie's Progress

Hello!, I'm back, it's me Marie
I've been a busy little bee
You know I joined a dating site?
Well I have just met Mr. Right!

He's handsome, tall, and very nice
He's so involved, we've been out twice!
Now I'm not one for rushing things
Like booking halls and buying rings.

I took him home to meet my Dad
And thinking back, I'm really glad
Daddy said, "You've made my day!
"Make sure he cannot get away!"

I thought that now I should propose
A little forward, I suppose
But when I got down on my knees
I'll swear I heard him say "Yes please!!"

So Mummy wants to wedding plan
To join Marie, and her new man
I know you all will be delighted
That's why you are all invited!

RSVP

Episode Nine: INVITATIONS

Mr. & Mrs. Capulet

Cordially invite all Poets to the marriage
ceremony of their daughter;

Marie Juliet Kylie Capulet

To:
Romeo Montgomery Elvis Montague.

The service will be held at 11:00 am at the
Church of Restoration and
Rehabilitation in Verona Sq. on Thursday
14th. February.

It is hoped that the service will be conduct-
ed by The Right Reverend Dr. Cotton Jones

(All rumours of De-Frocking are being
robustly defended in the courts)

Order of Service:

Hymn 267 Rock of Rages to the tune of
Thriller

Wedding Vows: Romeo has agreed to
'Obey' but is a little unhappy about the

'Body Worship' bit.

Marie has responded with
'We'll see about that.'

Hymn 381 Father, Son and Holy Goat to the
tune of Bat out of Hell.

Signing of the book of Registry in the Vestry
to be witnessed by
Seasofme and SloanRanger who have
insisted on crossing their fingers.

Seating: Montague party to the left,
Capulet party to the right.

All Poets attending the ceremony to be
seated behind the security glass
At the rear of the church.

This is to prevent the tossing of acrostics
and rhyming couplets
Which are known to be injurious to health.

The wedding breakfast is to be held
(By kind permission)
At the Wal-Mart Social club on balcony St.

Entertainment will be provided by Crimson
red, fronted by,

The inimitable Bill Temple. Crimson Red
were big in the sixties
Even bigger in the seventies, but in the
eighties were forced
To join weight watchers as finding clothes
had become impossible.

Once the festivities are over guests are
requested to leave quietly
Showing respect for close neighbours
Such as The Shakespeare Care Home for
penless Poets
And the Cemetery for literary greats

(Space must be booked in advance, all
writes reserved)

One final matter, the rumours of Dylan
attended are false
He is currently touring with
'Dying of the Light'

RSVP

Episode Ten: Marie's Hen Night

Sloanranger organised this bash
But truth to tell, she used my cash
I do not mind, she's such a dear
As long as she stays off the beer.

Fallen_Tear has just walked in
I think she must have hit the Gin
Her gait is wobbly and unsteady
She's headed for the bar already.

Lisaner says that she can't drink
She's got no cash is what I think
I'm not sure if that is true
I'll leave that one up to you.

Grapher's been here for a while
Gorgeous clothes and stunning smile
But I'm not fooled, she's devious
She's clever and mischievous.

Varruni's chatting up some guys
So's Sharon P that's no surprise
They carry on and there'll be trouble
"Oh, yes please, I'll have a double."

Gailrunschke looks sophisticated
Kristebelle.....inebriated
That Sara girl is quite alright
Been buying me some drinks tonight.

Knightwriter's not the only one
Who looks as if she's having fun
My head is feeling sort of furry
And my voice is kind of slurry.

Hindia and all her crowd
Are giggling and they're very loud
Hughena's drinking orange juice
Too much Vodka makes her loose.

I think I might call it a night
Before these Poets start to fight
Midnight's drawing very near
Don't want to leave my slipper here!!!

Episode Eleven: Marie's Wedding

Well, here we are, it's wedding day
With luck, Marie is on her way
Romeo's been here a while
Once, or twice, I've seen him smile.

His hair is combed, and highly waxed
He looks okay, in fact, relaxed
His best man doesn't look the same
I think Vernicho's his name.

He looks real tense and quite uptight
He says that he's been up all night
He's worried things will not go well
So am I, if truth to tell.

The Poets come, in ones, and twos
Some barefoot and some with shoes
They've made an effort to portray
Themselves as normal, for today.

Bill Temple's wearing morning dress
I think he's trying to impress
He sports a really tall top hat
Inside I'm sure I heard that cat.

You know, the one that writes a blog
And helps with poems about fog
But I suppose that it's alright
As long as he stays out of sight.

The poets seem to be quite quiet
Allaying fears of minor riot
If everything remains this way
We might just have a normal day.

Seasofme has made it here
Arm in arm with Fallentear
Knightwriter's sat with Kristebelle
Sloanranger's just crept in as well.

The organ strikes a mournful note
It sounds like something Temple wrote
But no, it is the wedding tune
Which means Marie will be here soon.

Yes, here she comes, a wondrous sight
Dressed from head to toe, in white
Looking happy, and so calm
She drags her father by the arm.

He looks stern, and rather grave
As all the poets shout and wave
But steadfastly he makes his way
Determined they'll not spoil the day.

The reverend Jones stands tall and proud
Points out the Poets, shouts out loud
"Please, you lot, be calm, collected
Or I'll have you all ejected!!"

He turns to Romeo, and bows
And reads the lad his wedding vows
"Do you take this girl, Marie?
"To love and cherish fervently?"

"I do, I do" cries Romeo
"He does, he does" says Vernicho
The preacher shakes his weary head
Attending to Marie instead.

"Will you also love and cherish
Romeo until you perish?"
"Oh yes, I'll love him all my days
"And cherish him in many ways!!"

"Okay, you two, that's quite enough
"I do not need to hear that stuff!!
"I now pronounce you man and wife
"And hope you have a happy life."

Marie's achieved her lifelong dream
As has her father, it would seem
They leave the church in love's embrace
A life together now to face.

The Poets now think it's all done
And they can really have some fun
Pads and pens just hit the air
Demonstrating they don't care.

Acrostics and a random thought
Means nothing now, it's all just nought
They love Marie, but think it should
Provide some copy, if it could.

They think the wedding breakfast might
Provide some interest, if they're right
There could be speeches, good and bad
They'll write them down, they'll not be sad.

Let's leave that for another day
And bless Marie, that's what I say
Let us hope that very soon
She'll just enjoy her honeymoon!!

Episode Twelve: Marie's Return

Hello folks, it's me Marie
I'm back from honeymoon you see
I thought that you would like to know
How my honeymoon did go.

My Romeo's a real stud
I guess it's his Italian blood
Within two nights we'd broke the bed
And had to use the floor instead!

Then it appears we were too loud
We had to leave under a cloud
So we went and bought a tent
Found a field and off we went.

Eventually we went to sleep
To be awoken by some sheep!!
Then the farmer came to say
He wanted us to go away.

So we caught an aeroplane
Now we are back home again
We really need somewhere to live
Is there some help that you can give.

One of you must have some space
A nice and warm and sound-proofed place
We'd be good tenants, pay the rent
To settle down is our intent.

You're only Poets after all
Your need for space must be quite small
Give your address to Owain Glyn
We'll be right round and move right in!!!

ABOUT THE AUTHOR

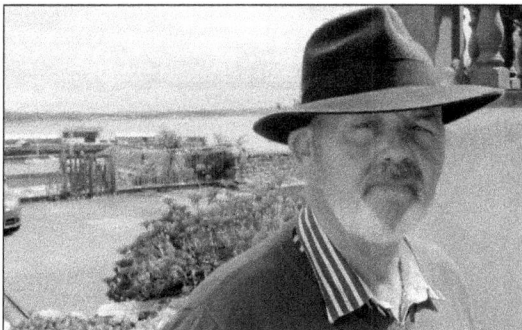

Owain Glyn is a Welsh exile currently living on the wild Atlantic coast in the U.K. His love of language and his need to observe drives him to write on a wide variety of subjects. One of his favourite is 'Humour,' the ability to see the funny side of life goes a long way to relieve stress and improve mental health. He hopes the reader will smile along with him.

This collection is dedicated to his Grandson Jack.

www.ingramcontent.com/pod-product-compliance
Lightning Source LLC
Chambersburg PA
CBHW060535030426
42337CB00021B/4279